THIS BOOK IS DEDICATED TO ALL PEOPLE WHO HAVE HELPED AND MOTIVATED ME THROUGHOUT MY LIFE, ESPECIALLY MY PARENTS AND MY BROTHER

A COLLECTION OF SHORT STORIES & ESSAYS

(FOR MIDDLE AND HIGH SCHOOL)

WRITTEN BY:

HAMMAD FAROOQUI

Copyright Reserved by the Author

First Edition: 2017

© All Rights Reserved. No part of this e-book may be reproduced in any form without prior written permission of the author. The author, since childhood, has worked very hard in producing the contents of this e-book.

Persons found dealing in pirated version of this e-book will be strictly dealt with. To avoid purchase of sub-standard pirated version, insist on taking a receipt. Your support and guidance in this regard will be highly appreciated and will help us serve you better.

Price: $3.99

Disclaimer: This book is meant for enlightening students and to help them in essay and story writing. The contents in no way whatsoever violate any existing copyrights or intellectual property rights and the names used in the compositions are a work of fiction, bearing no resemblance to any object, company or person either dead or alive; nor does it intend to portray anyone in bad light.

PREFACE

Essay writing is an art. It's an art through which your words can bring up a world of their own , give your reason a voice, make your opinions count and heard and most importantly give you the freedom to express your imagination, feelings, knowledge and facts.

'A Collection of Short Stories & Essays' is a compilation of passages, stories and essays that I have been writing for the past 9-10 years. As a child, I was taught meticulously the way of essay writing both at home and school. Over the years, the amount of essays I had with me kept piling up till I one day decided to type them all out and publish them so that the world can get to read them.

Many people struggle to reproduce the ideas they have in their minds and do justice to their imagination. English being our second language and perhaps the most used language in the world can sometimes prove difficult to most of us when it comes to being creative with it. This motivated me to come up with a student friendly book that could set the wheels of imagination into a motion in the right direction. Plus, as a student myself I understand how and what the students require in a book such as this. The purpose of this book is to provide people with a wide range of essays which are frequently asked in various schools' and colleges' examinations. The students can quickly go through the essays, take an idea of what it is expected to be there in an essay and then freely wield their pens in the exam hall. Not only during the examination can these compositions be useful, but also can provide a good read during leisure hours.

I hope this book will hit the right notes with the minds of our youth, unleash their expressive talent and help them at every step of their educational career.

INDEX

1.	I was alone in the house when the doorbell rang	12
2.	An Accident I witnessed	14
3.	A day when everything went wrong	16
4.	A dark and stormy night	18
5.	A House on Fire	20
6.	A mysterious telephone call	22
7.	A Terrifying Experience	24
8.	On your first plane, the plane catches fire. Describe your experience	26
9.	A pleasant surprise	28
10.	An amazing incident	30
11.	The Honest Driver	32
12.	A story ending with '_____then it burst into flames.'	36
13.	A story on three miners trapped inside a mine,	39

	waiting for rescue or death	
14.	An Adventure	46
15.	A Street Accident	49
16.	Imagine you have sprouted wings and can fly. Describe how you felt at first. What you did and any adventures that you had in the one day that you were given wings	52
17.	As I turned on my bed____	56
18.	A Brave Deed	60
19.	Escape	63
20.	Honesty is the best policy	66
21.	An Interesting Journey	69
22.	You are alone at home one evening studying for a unit test when all at once you hear a knocking sound	72
23.	"Through my semi-conscious state I heard distant peals of a	75

	telephone bell ringing_____"	
24.	Write a story on a bank robbery	79
25.	Write an original story where there is sudden panic on the streets with men shouting, women screaming and people running helter-skelter. What has caused this situation and how it is solved and what should be the subject of the story?	83
26.	Write an interesting story beginning with- 'three men found a purse full of gold coins while walking through a forest.'	86
27.	You were at an event attended by thousands of people. Give a detailed description of the event and tell us what you did, thought	89

	and felt in the large crowd	
28.	Rivalry	94
29.	A robbery in a running train	98
30.	A meeting with a ghost	101
31.	My Greatest Wish	104
32.	A story based on the theme: Knowledge is Power	107
33.	Write a short story on: You cannot climb the ladder of success with hands in your pocket	111
34.	A story on a rivalry between a father and son	114
35.	A meeting with an alien	118

I WAS ALONE IN THE HOUSE WHEN THE DOORBELL RANG

I was alone in the house. My parents had gone to an official dinner. I had my Geography test the next day and was trying hard to concentrate on the vegetation and climate of Australia.

Suddenly the doorbell rang. I jumped out of my chair as I was not expecting anyone at 9:30 p.m. to be precise. I cautiously opened the door and saw a man of average height with black moustache standing outside. He thrust an ID into my face and said in a heavy voice, "I am Inspector Singh from S.T.F. I have received information that a notorious criminal Kalka has thrown a stolen bag of jewels in your house while fleeing from the police." I looked at him in disbelief. The inspector produced a warrant to search my house. He then proceeded to make a thorough search of the garden. He looked under each bush and behind every tree. He searched the courtyard and ransacked the veranda. He turned everything upside down. He then proceeded towards the servant quarter. After a few minutes Mr. Singh shouted, "I have found it..... It's here! I knew it!" I hurriedly entered the servant quarter to see what he had discovered. To my astonishment he was holding a bag containing the dirty toys of my maid's daughter. I tried to tell him but he would not understand. When he finally looked inside the bag he was disappointed. He muttered that he was sure the thief had dropped the bag at house number- M-14. I suddenly stopped and told him that this isn't M-14 but N-14. On hearing this he dashed off.

Whenever I picture the Inspector's face I burst out laughing.

AN ACCIDENT I WITNESSED

Thousands of people die in road accidents every year. Most of the accidents take place due to rash and careless driving. People do not follow the traffic rules properly.

One day I was going with my father in a car to school. It were morning hours and everyone was in hurry to reach their destination. There was a traffic jam near Cathedral school. A young man on a motorcycle behind us was in a great hurry. He was driving very fast. At the crossing he tried to overtake others in front of us. In this attempt, he hit a rickshaw carrying school children. The rickshaw driver fell down and his rickshaw overturned. The children fell down. One school boy hit his head on a stone lying on the road. He instantly became unconscious. He was bleeding profusely.

The other children also got seriously hurt. They were all crying. It was a terrible sight. My father stopped the car at the roadside and we got down.

A large crowd had gathered. Some of them tried to help the injured children. Some others caught the motor-cycle rider and tried to thrash him. A policeman appeared on the scene and the motor cycle rider was handed over to him. My father meanwhile took all the injured children to a nearby civil hospital. We even called the children's parents. I was horrified and badly shaken by this accident. We left the hospital with a heavy heart.

These accidents prove disastrous and end in terrible loss of life and property. Reckless drivers should be punished severely. Traffic rules should be followed strictly and road sense should be developed from a very young age.

A DAY WHEN EVERYTHING WENT WRONG

There is a day that we would like to forget. A day in which nothing right seemed to happen. Till today, I have nightmares recalling the day and wish I do not have to relive the same again.

It was the second of August and I was sleeping soundly when the electricity went off. To my discomfort the inverter failed to start. I got up sweating five o' clock in the morning. Then as I was going to school, the car tyre got punctured. I was late and the prefects made me take ten rounds of the field. I was cursing my ill stars for the humiliation. On reaching my class I took my seat and settled down. My class teacher started taking the math test. I was dumbstruck as I had not prepared for it. Yesterday my friend had told me on the phone that today was the English test.

I glared at him for misleading me. I had missed my classes as I had to go for my debate practices and the earth seemed to slip beneath me as I tried to come to terms with this tragedy. To give the test without any preparation was a nightmare. I however gathered my wits and began to attempt the questions with trembling hands.

During the recess period as soon as I opened my lunch box all the food dropped to the floor and I had to remain hungry. Tears filled my eyes. As if this was not enough, I was punished for not bringing my science book and was asked to stand outside the class. I heaved a sigh of relief on hearing the toll of the school bell.

    It was the worst day of my life and I still have illusions of this nightmare. Recalling it sends a shiver down my spine.

A DARK AND STORMY NIGHT

It was a dark and stormy night when suddenly I heard "Help! Help!" from outside my window. It sounded like my neighbour, old Dr. Chandra. I wondered what the matter was. Then the shout for help came again.

This time I grabbed an umbrella and dashed over to Dr. Chandra's workplace to find out why he was shouting for help. My father was right behind me.

We found him sitting in his veranda, one hand holding the other limp hand. He was groaning in pain. Mrs. Chandra was seated next to him. The wind was howling and it was raining cats and dogs. Flashes of lightning and sounds of thunder could be seen and heard. We wondered what Dr. Chandra was doing in his lawn in such a stormy weather. "What's the matter?" I asked him. He said," I was bitten by something, maybe a snake". My father immediately brought out his car and we helped Dr. Chandra get into it. Then we sped to the hospital about two kilometers away. It was hard and difficult to drive because the rain was coming down heavily. The trees were swaying in the wind and the roads were littered with leaves and suddenly a tree fell on the road near a crossing. We were lucky that our car had just passed that place otherwise we would have been stuck for ages.

On the way to the hospital Dr. Chandra told us that he had gone to the lawn to pick the clothes lying on the line to dry. He bent on the grass to pick a few clothes that had fallen when something bit him. The pain in his index finger was excruciating. It was swollen and there was a bite mark on it.

At the hospital we helped him into the emergency room where he was attended by a doctor. It was a painful ordeal for Dr. Chandra but he recovered. He is back home but neither he nor us can forget that dark stormy night and how with great difficulty we drove to the hospital.

A HOUSE ON FIRE

Fire has many advantages and disadvantages. It gives us heat and light but sometimes it can be destructive.

A few days back I was going to the market when I saw a palatial two-storey house on fire. Thick smoke was coming out of the doors and windows. I could see the flames shooting high in the sky: A strong wind was fanning the flames. A crowd had gathered in front of the house which belonged to a certain Mr. Gupta. A few family members were trapped inside and were crying for help. People with pails and buckets were running towards the house trying their best to douse the flames. Some were throwing sand on the flames. The inmates of the house looked gloomy and sad.

Soon the fire-brigade rushed towards the house. The firemen quickly pulled the hosepipes and started squirting water on the shooting flames. They wore fire proof uniform, bright brass helmets on their heads and long boots. A few firemen put up ladders against the wall to save the people caught inside. One of the firemen brought a child safely out of the house. He again went to rescue the others.

It took more than an hour to control the fire. There were heavy losses. The house was badly damaged. Two women received serious burn injuries. They were rushed to a nearby hospital. The cause of the fire was due to short circuit. It was the most horrifying scene that I had ever witnessed.

A MYSTERIOUS TELEPHONE CALL

It was Saturday night and my father and I were watching a Jackie Chan movie. It was late at night when suddenly the telephone started ringing. Reluctantly I picked it up. A faint weak voice came from the other side. "Hello uncle Amaan please help me." It was the voice of a small boy. I told him that he had dialed the wrong number. The boy started to cry. I asked the boy which number he had dialed and he said 40033808 and I knew it was a mistake as my number was 40033809. I asked him the problem. In a terrified voice he said that some thieves had entered his house. They had locked his parents in one room and his sister and him in another. In a hurry they had not seen the mobile phone lying on the sofa.

I quickly asked the boy's address and disconnected the phone. My father was listening to our conversation. When I told him the problem, he immediately called up his friend who happened to be the SSP of the area. He gave the address and requested that the police be at once rushed there. With a few police personnel we all bundled in a jeep and rushed to the boy's house. The police parked the jeep a few meters away and surrounded the house. They took their positions and at once pounced on the thieves when they came out of the house with the booty.

The four thieves were arrested. They had planned the robbery with help of the servant of the house. Now they had to live in the jail. The boy and his parents were very thankful to us. It was past midnight when we went to bed. Had I ignored the mysterious call, it would have led to a serious tragedy.

A TERRIFYING EXPERIENCE

There are some incidents which one never forgets in life. Some incidents are pleasant and some are terrifying.

I remember, during my last summer holidays, I had gone to visit my aunt who lives in Mumbai. Her old rambling house is on the beach. My mother had strictly forbidden me not to go to the beach alone. One day my cousins wanted to play football. They called me to join them. I quickly tiptoed out of the house. I was muttering to myself that if my mother finds out, I will be in big trouble. No one saw me going. I raced at top speed in my swimming trunks. We started playing football happily. Suddenly my cousin kicked the ball. The tide came in and carried the ball further away from the shore. I wanted to show off my swimming skills so I decided to retrieve the ball all by myself. I dived into the sea. After swimming for a while, I became tried. When I saw the ball was a few feet away from me, I put an extra effort. That very moment, my feet got tangled in some seaweed. I struggled to keep afloat, but it was in vain. I screamed and shouted for help, but no one came. After a while I fainted.

When I woke up, I was lying in a room. A doctor walked in and then I realized that I was in a hospital. My mother half angry and half-worried came with the doctor.

Thankfully they were no serious injuries. It was the most terrifying experience of my life.

ON YOUR FIRST PLANE JOURNEY THE PLANE CATCHES FIRE. DESCRIBE THE INCIDENT

This summer vacation my family decided to go to Hong Kong We got our flight seats booked a week in advance. It was my first air trip and I was very excited and happy. I found the idea of flying like a bird in the sky, strange and wonderful.

Our plane took off from Indira Gandhi International Airport on the 26th of May at 9am. Before the take-off, all the passengers went for security check. We took our boarding pass and soon we were seated inside with our seat belts fastened. When the plane started moving on the run way, there was a terrific noise. In no time it left the ground and started flying. I felt a little giddy and my ears seemed to swell. As I looked down I could see trees, houses and vehicles on the road. They all seemed like toys. Suddenly the fire alarm rang out. The aero-plane's tail had caught fire. All the passengers started to panic. Some were screaming and crying. The air hostess asked everyone to wear the life jackets. The plane started losing height. It was coming very fast to the ground. The pilot alerted the airport authorities for an emergency landing. I was crying and praying to God. We thought that this was the end. We were all going to die. All the passengers were quickly taken to the emergency exits. The plane landed with a loud noise. The rear of the plane was in flames. We inflated our life jackets and jumped out of the emergency exits. The fire brigade was already there extinguishing the fire. Some passengers already had severe burn injuries. With a loud noise the plane split into two.

We were all taken in an ambulance to a hospital. My family was one of the lucky ones to have survived with just a few bruises. More than thirty people died in the plane crash. My first trip turned out to be a nightmare. It was the most terrifying experience of my life.

A PLEASANT SURPRISE

Life is full of surprises. Sometimes it is a happy one and at other times full of sorrow. The happy ones are always cherished by us and imbibed in our memories forever. It is impossible to forget them.

Since the past few years, I had been asking my parents for a very hi-tech gaming toy, but time after time they turned down my request saying I was too young to play with hi-tech gaming toys and should rather focus on traditional computer games and other sports like cricket, football and badminton. But it just happened last month, my father was on his business trip to Singapore. He came across the just launched Sony PSP, a hand held gaming toy. He asked me via e-mail if I wanted one and by past experience, I was not excited at all, assuming this would never really happen. But when my father arrived in Lucknow, he presented me with this state of the art gaming toy from Sony. I just could not believe that I was holding world's latest gizmo in my hand with all the latest games installed in it. This was a pleasant surprise which I had never expected from my parents. My PSP had everything latest in it. It could connect to Wi-Fi, computer and play games with other users and even surf the net. I could also download the latest games from the Internet. This pleasant surprise increased my love for my parents.

I really thank God for giving me such wonderful parents and also all the good things in life that he has blessed me with. It is a gift that I will cherish forever.

AN AMUSING INCIDENT

An amusing incident happened in my life a few years back. It was a cloudy morning in July. The lanes around my neighborhood were wet and slippery. It was my cousin's birthday and he had been gifted a wonderful new racing bike.

Now, this cousin of mine is ten years older to me. He fancied he was a future Olympic cycling champion, able to ride in all conditions and at all kinds of speed. He was skinny and athletic and a daredevil. "Come on!" he shouted as I stood admiring his bike. He asked me to hop on front and he'll take me for a spin.

I was only eight years old then and I couldn't resist the invitation. Soon we were speeding out on the streets, which were in some places water logged.

It was quiet that day. There was not much traffic on the road. We overlook a few cars which were travelling very slowly and carefully. Our bicycle was however speeding down like the speed of light or so it seemed to me. A few times I shrieked at my cousin to slow down as I wanted to get off. He ignored my appeal and went faster. We were rocketing along when we came to a sharp bend. My cousin applied the brakes and the bicycle skidded on the wet road and we were thrown into a puddle of dirty water. I was very angry at him.

I can now see the funny side of the incident. My cousin and I laugh when we remember it. I have never been out on a bike with him again, though.

THE HONEST DRIVER

It was very hot in May and my summer vacation had just started. I was getting bored at home as I had nothing to do. My father had to go to Singapore on a business trip. When he asked me out of the blue whether I would like to accompany him, I jumped with excitement.

We started making plans as to all the beautiful and enchanting places we would see. I had heard a lot about Singapore. It is one of the most beautiful cities in the world and has a lot to offer to the tourists. My father applied for the visa and one fine morning we caught our flight from New Delhi's Indira Gandhi International Airport. It was a six hour journey. When we landed at the Changi Airport, my joy knew no bounds. I was ecstatic.

We hired a taxi to take us to our hotel which was located in Little India. On our way I kept looking at the tall buildings, the river front and the fast moving traffic. I was enraptured and kept chatting and asking my father when would it be possible for us to visit the city Zoo, as I wanted to have a photograph clicked with an orangutan.

When we got down from the taxi and entered the lobby of our hotel, my father realized that he had left his bag containing our passports, traveler's cheque and cash in the taxi. The hotel receptionist asked us whether we knew the taxi number. To our dismay we realized we had hardly noticed the taxi number. Then she asked us the color of the taxi. "It was blue," we replied. She was most helpful and told us that all the blue colored taxis belonged to one particular company. She told us the address of the company which thankfully was close by. We walked to their office as we had no money. The company official radioed to all his taxis if any of the drivers had seen a black leather bag containing two Indian passports, cash and travelers' cheque. For two hours we waited with bated breath and kept praying to God fervently. Again the company radioed to all its employees asking them again to recheck.

After more than three hours of endless wait and despair we got the message that the taxi driver whose taxi we had hired had left the bag at his company's counter at the airport. He probably thought that the travelers will come back to the airport from where they had hired the taxi, looking for their missing valuables.

We felt relieved. Our nightmare had finally ended. The honest driver had not given in to temptation. The bag had not been touched. All our passports and money was there. We thanked the company and the driver profusely. Had it not been for their honesty and sincerity we would have been left stranded in a foreign land with no money and no place to go. We tried to reward the driver by giving him our watch and money but he refused to take it. He told us that he was only doing his duty and said that the only way he could be rewarded was to spread the message of honesty and hospitality of people of Singapore in India.

A STORY ENDING WITH:

...THEN IT BURST INTO FLAMES.

Mr. Craig, the President of United States of America had just finished addressing the United Nations on the war against terrorism. He spoke about his country's stand on the situation in Afghanistan, Iraq and Syria. He continued to defend the involvement of his country in carrying out strikes against the terrorists and he pledged to show the terrorists that he and his nation were not afraid of them.

To fulfill his promise, he decided to visit the war zones of Iraq and Afghanistan to boost the morale of the U.S. troops. His decision was widely criticized by everyone. Many famous and reputed leaders of the world warned him not to endanger his life but no one was able to convince him. Preparations of his arrival had begun in full swing. Cameras were being installed on the streets. The airport had become a no flying zone and all the other flights were cancelled. Vehicles were being checked and scanned. The roads had to be deserted and a team of FBI agents had arrived a week ago to ensure that the security measures met their requirements.

The news of his coming was not met positively by the people. They led a strong demonstration of their views, burned his posters and carried out protests in front of the U.S. embassy. They believed that his policies were doing them more harm than the terrorists. The terrorists also released a video putting a bounty on Craig for a million US dollars and promised to carry out attacks against him and his troops.

The president arrived in Baghdad. Unfortunately due to shortage of time his car could not be transported.

The President was accompanied by his agents and defense officers and were greeted by the men of his army and officers representing the President of Iraq. He was given a convoy of ten vehicles and many convoys identical to this were already on the move. This was done to fool anyone who wanted to carry out any type of attack.

Soon they reached the outskirts of the battlefield where he met Sergeant Paul who explained Harvey their progress in war against terrorism. Harvey shared a cup of tea with the troops before going to another war front. Snipers were placed in buildings and on rooftops. People had sprayed bad words against the U.S. government on the walls. Two or three men in their youth were walking on the streets and were quickly arrested by the police. The President visited the different war zones where his troops were posted and then decided to return to the airport.

As the convoys were moving people defied the orders of the police and rushed onto the streets. The snipers could neither get a clear view nor could they shoot any innocent civilian. The police then rushed with clubs to disperse them. The security men of the convoy tried to scatter the people. Under ten minutes the streets were clear of civilians and the main car in convoy moved a bit and then it burst into flames.

A STORY ON: THREE MINERS TRAPPED IN A MINE, WAITING FOR RESCUE OR DEATH.

Mukesh was the only son of his parents. He had to look after his four sisters and when his father got diagnosed with cancer he had to stop his studies and he took up a job as a miner in Hazaribagh copper mines. His early days were tough; the person who supervised mining was a nasty rude fellow who used to make the minors work in terrible conditions.

Mukesh was always helped by Mohan who had run away from home to escape his abusive father. Mohan lived near the mining area and knew everything about the mines. One day as the miners were mining there was an explosion.

All the miners had left for lunch break. Mukesh, Mohan and another minor were close to the ramps leading to the surface but suddenly they heard an explosion and the ramps leading to the surface collapsed.

Suresh, the third miner trapped inside was an insolent person who always picked up fights with his fellow miners. No one knew about his personal life.

All the connections to the surface had been cut. Electricity had gone and they were 2,000 feet beneath the Earth's surface with no food and water. Mukesh and Mohan tried their best to find a way to escape but all their efforts went in vain. Suresh did nothing and cursed his luck. Somehow they managed to make their way to the refuge chamber where they spent the entire night. No one uttered a word to each other. Meanwhile the government had started operations to rescue them. People started raising questions about whether the mines follow the standard safety regulations or not. The Prime Minister assured the families of the miners that they would rescue them at all cost.

In the morning the trapped miners began to find a way to quench their thirst.

Mohan knew that thousand of liters of water kept the engines of their machinery cool. When they took out the water Suresh demanded to have it for himself as life had been unfair for him. He was always deprived of things and he wanted to survive to prove himself worthy and to become successful. After a short fight they subdued him and were kind enough to offer him the dirty, oily water which was drinkable enough to keep them alive. They sat in the darkness with the lights of their helmet on.

Suresh for the first time spoke about his troubled past. Mohan and Mukesh were surprised to hear that he was an outstanding student and a graduate but was unable to find any job and as a result failed to repay the loans which he had taken in order to complete his education. His father was a retired clerk in a government institution and his pension could not support the family. Suresh thought he had failed himself and his family. Mohan also spoke about losing his mother at a very young age. How his father had lost everything in gambling and the ordeal which his father subjected upon him when he was drunk. Mohan told the whole incidence of how he ran away from home and the three realized that how miserable circumstances can be.

The first day was about to pass, they had not eaten anything and were surviving on the machine water and the oxygen level was going down. The sound of their coughing was so loud due to the echo of the mine that they mistook it for another explosion. They prayed and went to sleep but were haunted by the memories of their family and loved ones. The rescue teams came up with a plan to rescue them in the shortest time possible. Mukesh could not stop thinking about his dying father and his sisters and he started undergoing hypertension. The machine water was ruining their health. Suresh's leg had swollen up and Mohan developed the first symptoms of pneumonia.

The media dubbed their survival chance less than 1%. Due to starvation they had problems of temporary blindness. They had not seen the sunlight for two days and when they heard the sound of drilling they became overjoyed. Music was their only past time. Mohan's health was deteriorating and Suresh's watch had stopped working.

They could hear the sound of drilling nearby but never knew when they would be rescued. They began to imagine things and when one of the drills broke through to the men they thought it was an underground creature that would kill them. Soon they realized that the rescue teams had come and they were going to be rescued. The three of them were neither happy nor excited; they just wanted a good meal to eat and clean drinking water to drink. The rescue workers carried them out. Mohan was rushed into an ambulance. Suresh and Mukesh broke down on seeing the light again and the medics came to examine them.

The Prime Minster met the miners and announced a healthy reward for their bravery. He appreciated the work of everyone who was involved in this operation and said if the miners had been trapped more deep inside the mine then it would not have been possible to rescue them on time.

AN ADVENTURE

It was midnight when suddenly the lights went off. It became incredibly pitch dark followed by an eerie silence. I was all alone at home. My parents had gone for an official party, leaving me to struggle doggedly with my lessons.

I lay in my bed and pulled the covers over my head. My heart started beating fast, and my hands become cold and clammy. My throat dried up as I heard a horrible high pitched sound of something sliding across my bedroom floor, inch by inch coming closer to my bed. I cried out "Who's there?" from beneath my covers light gripping my pillow tightly. An evil laugh echoed throughout my room as the sound came closer.

I was petrified with fear. My mind became blank. I felt as if my heart beat had stopped. Through the blankets I could see an outstretched hand coming towards me. "No, no, go away!" I screamed as the hand came closer. "This is it!" I muttered out loud "This is the end!" I shot straight up in my bed, still screaming, shaking and breathing heavily when I finally convinced myself it was a dream. Panting heavily I tried to look at my clock and with difficulty found that it was past one o' clock. The dream that had been giving me goose bumps for days, even weeks had returned. As I sat there shaking, the memories of the Boogeyman and the stories that my older cousin told me about him, slowly seeped into my head, without a way of being dislodged. My flesh was crawling as cold shivers ran up and down my spine. My hair stood on end. I tried my hardest to go back to sleep, but I tossed and turned for what seemed like hours but were only minutes. "That's it!" I sputtercd out loud, "I can't keep doing this."

I gathered courage in both my hands to face the Boogeyman. I reluctantly kicked away the covers and swung my feet to the side of the bed. Rubbing my eyes so that I could see clearly, I reached for the drawer of my side table. I pulled out a small flashlight. My feet hit the cold floor and my legs almost gave up as I tried to stand up. I decided to be my father's son. I wanted to make sure that the Boogeyman was not in my room. I looked underneath my bed and inside my closet and a sigh of relief escaped me as nothing popped out of it at me and I realized that the Boogeyman was not in my room.

Suddenly, I heard a knock on the door and instantly my growing courage changed into fear. My heart sank in my shoes. But it was not the Boogeyman, they were my parents. They scolded me for being awake for so long in the night but when I narrated the whole episode to them, they praised me for my bravery. As I lay in my bed, it hit me that the Boogeyman wasn't real and I realized that all the stories that my elder cousin had told me were made up to scare me. "Ah-h!" I sighed, "I can't wait until tomorrow."

A STREET ACCIDENT

One pleasant evening my friend Tusshar and I sat on the high grass embankment beside the main road near our house. It was quite safe to sit on the embankment and watch the traffic go by. We played our favourite game of car-naming, that is, to correctly identify any approaching vehicle.

The stretch of road were we sat was straight and cars that passed by travelled fast and a number of bad accidents had already occurred on this stretch. Signs were put to warn the motorists, but they did not seem to make much difference.

From where we were sitting, we saw two cars racing at breakneck speed down the road. One was trying to overtake the other and it was obvious that none of them had any intention of giving way. Side by side, they roared down the road. They whizzed past where we sat at a speed of about 130km/h. Tusshar and I were on our feet gaping at the spectacle below.

From the opposite direction a huge lorry suddenly appeared. I heard a loud screeching sound as the car that was trying to overtake skidded and knocked into the other car. The driver of one of the cars must have panicked and applied the brakes on seeing the lorry. The two cars moved together for a short distance and then separated. One climbed the embankment for a while and then toppled backwards, lending on its roof, crumbling it. The other car grazed along the embankment for a long agonizing moment before coming to rest with its left side completely ripped off.

Suddenly all was quiet. The scene was awesome. The smoke filled air smelled of burnt oil and rubber. The sight of twisted metal and flames coming from beneath the bonnet of one of the cars was enough to nauseate anybody. We stood rooted to the ground, spellbound and frightened. Then we ran to where the cars were. There was no sign of life. The lorry's driver and attendant ran to help the victims. The driver of the car whose roof was crushed was dead. Fortunately for the driver whose side was damaged was alive but badly bruised and bleeding. We tried to help him out of the car but his safety belt was jammed. The lorry driver had a knife which he used to cut the driver free.

Meanwhile other cars arrived and presently the police and an ambulance came. The ambulance took the injured man to the hospital.

It was already dark when we made our way home. I could not sleep well that night and kept dreaming about the accident. The next morning I just sat thinking of the dangers of reckless driving. We never sat on the embankment ever again.

IMAGINE THAT YOU HAVE SPROUTED WINGS AND CAN FLY. DESCRIBE HOW YOU FELT AT FIRST. WHAT YOU DID AND ANY ADVENTURES THAT YOU HAD

IN THE ONE DAY THAT YOU WERE GIVEN WINGS

What a day it was! It all began the previous night when I felt something coming out of me, making it impossible for me to sleep. I was trembling with fear and I shot up from my bed panting heavily.

Something heavy was on my back. I was really curious to kill that thing for it had disturbed my sleep.

I tried to hit it with my hand but shockingly, the very sort of creature hit me on my back, too. It felt dejected. I switched on my room lights, and ran to the side mirror. The reflection of my image in the mirror slowly changed my fear and anger into happiness, as I discovered that I had sprouted wings. I was so surprised. They hung around me just as an angel with its beautiful feathers.

As I moved my triceps and biceps, the wings too moved swiftly making a rustling sound with the wind. I ran to my bedroom window. I took notice of the time. The hands of the clock had joined each other. It was midnight.

Little frightened but even more excited to test my newly grown wings, I jumped out of the window, flapped them, closed my eyes and even before that I could imagine how I was about to crash land, I zapped through the air. It was a memorable experience. Lucknow looked so beautiful from the air. Only the street lights were on, and I could see some cars of the size of ants ambling their way. I was feeling at the top of the world. Later, dawn arrived carrying with it beautiful pale golden rays of the rising sun. What a sight it was as I sat on the topmost branches of a tree looking at it. The reflection of light from the mirrors of the buildings entered my eyes and the sparkling water of the river Gomti made the sight even more scintillating. Later, a flock of birds flew above me and I too decided to join them. I was so engrossed with them that I forgot that my parents must be worrying about me. I decided to part with nature and went back to the urban life to which I belonged. My parents too, were surprised to see my wings.

I told them about my adventures with the beauties of Nature. They decided to keep me at home rather than send me to school. What problems I had at home! I couldn't enter my store room because my wings had made me broad. I was unable to eat my lunch because as I moved my hand my wing's feathers came on my mouth. So, my wings proved to be a nuisance as well.

At night again, I faced the gigantic problem of sleeping. I had no other option rather than to sleep while standing. I could not even sit because of my wings. I was feeling so dejected. Again, at midnight while leaning on the wall of my room, I felt the same pain which I had felt when my wings were coming out. Slowly, they disappeared and I finally hit the bed. I never ever wanted to be a bird again.

Although I could never forget my experience as a bird I realized and thanked God that human beings are the most advanced creatures.

AS I TURNED ON MY BED............

I heard a horrible, high- pitched sound of something sliding across my bedroom floor, inch by inch coming closer to my bed. I pulled the covers over my head, trembling with fear. The light outside my window pierced the incredible pitch- black darkness in my room. The light cast shadows onto my wall and my mind began to turn the shadows into terrible things.

"Who's there?" I cried out from beneath my covers, gripping my pillow with all my might. An evil laugh echoed throughout my room, as the sound came closer. Through the blankets, I could see an out stretched hand coming towards me. "No, no, go away!" I screamed as the hand came closer. "This is it!" I muttered out loud, "This is the end!"

I shot straight up in my bed still screaming, shaking and breathing heavily when I finally convinced myself it was a dream. Panting heavily, I looked at my clock and with difficulty found that it was past one o" clock. The dream that had been haunting me for days, even weeks, had returned. As I sat there shaking, the memories of the boogey man and the stories that my older cousin told me about him, slowly seeped into my head. I sat, still shaking, afraid to move even a muscle. I glanced around the room, which seemed much larger in the dark than it did during the daytime.

I tried my hardest to go back to sleep but I tossed and turned for what seemed like hours but were only minutes. "That's it", I sputtered out loud, "I can't keep doing this."

I reluctantly kicked away the covers and swung my feet to the side of the bed. Rubbing my eyes so that I could see clearly, I reached for the drawer of my side table. I pulled out a small flashlight. My feet hit the cold floor and my legs almost gave out as I tried to stand up. I wanted to make sure that the Boogey Man was not in my room. I slowly turned to face my bed and prepared myself to look underneath it. I turned on the torch as I bent over and lifted up the bed sheet. 'Thank God", I said with a sigh of relief. Then I spun around to face my closet. I slowly began to make my way towards the closet door. When I opened the door another sigh of relief escaped me when nothing popped out at me and I realized that the boogey man was not in my closet.

I made my way back to my bed and crawled back underneath the covers when I started to think about the stories that my cousin told me. Just then it hit me that the boogey man wasn't real. Something clicked and the light bulb in my head went off as I realized that all the stories that he told me were made up to scare me.

"Ahh," I sighed, "I can't wait until tomorrow."

A BRAVE DEED

Life is full of bad as well as good incidents. Some of them may be forgotten with the passage of time whereas others leave on everlasting imprint on the mind. It was a holiday. My cousin had come from New Delhi. My parents decided to go for a picnic to the Indira Canal. Soon we got ready and sped off in our car towards the picnic spot.

It was a pleasant day and the wind was flowing gently. When we reached the picnic spot, the place was humming with activity. The banks of the canal were occupied by holiday makers. We spread our straw mat that we had brought, under the shade of the tree. It was wonderful to just sit and relax and listen to the music. We ate the sandwiches and snacks we had got to our hearts' content. In the meantime, a few boys arrived very excited and began to change to get into the water as quickly as possible. They leapt into the cool water of the canal amidst yells of joy and laughter. They went about playing in the water for some time, splashing water at one another. Then all of a sudden we heard a scream. We looked up and saw that one of the boys was drowning. He was crying for help.

I immediately jumped into the water and swam towards the boy, not bothering to take my clothes off nor did I think of my own safety. I soon swam to the place where I had seen the boy. The boy had in the meantime been carried far away by the strong current. He was gasping for breath. At last I overtook the boy and caught him by the neck. The boy clung to me. I made for the bank as best I could. It was really difficult but I did not lose heart. I kept praying to God to help me. At last I reached the bank exhausted and completely out of breath. I dragged the boy on the bank and then sank on the ground. I lay in that state for some time. Mean while other people present there rushed to give the boy first-aid. He was given artificial respiration and he regained consciousness after a few minutes.

The boy's friends sat forlornly near me. They were full of remorse as they had forced the boy for a swim. Meanwhile my family and others present at the site surrounded me. They praised me for my brave deed. The boy's friends thanked me profusely for the courageous act as well. I was happy I had saved the boy from the jaws of death. The day would go down as one of the happiest days of my life. I have no doubt that God had inspired me to do this courageous deed.

ESCAPE

Mukesh, a young boy of about eighteen years of age with an average height and a dusky complexion, was on his way to college. His house was in a village in Sitapur District and he had come to Lucknow to pursue higher education.

One day he met a young man, about his own age. The man with a polite smile asked Mukesh where he was going. Not used to speaking to strangers, Mukesh ignored him, but the man kept talking. He said he was from Nindura, a village not for from Sitapur and his name was Sonu. Mukesh at once stopped in his tracks for he too was from the same village. They two soon became friends.

About a month later Sonu invited Mukesh to Begum Hazrat Mahal Park. The two strolled together, chatting. Then Sonu lead Mukesh round a cover to a large building where a door opened quietly as though they were expected.

Two men appeared from a dark passage and seized Mukesh by the arms. All pretence of politeness was dropped as Sonu's face turned harsh. He signalled the men to lock Mukesh.

Mukesh was held captive in a small room on the third floor of the building. There was only one tiny window which too was bolted. At first Mukesh was too stunned to react. Then he calmed down a bit and started thinking of ways to escape. Suddenly the door opened and a well built man wearing a dhoti and a kurta entered. He was the Gram Pradhan of his village. He spoke harshly, "You are a prisoner here. Tell your father to withdraw his nomination. If he fights the election against me, I will kill you. Saying this he pointed his revolver at Mukesh. Laughing aloud he went out.

Mukesh was trapped. He could not shout at the passersby for help as wooden boards were fastened across the window. His last chance was to appeal to the boy who came each day to clean his room and bring him food. Mukesh spoke to the boy, "I am innocent. My only crime is that my father is fighting the Gram Pradhan election against these people, please, help me and inform the police or else they will kill me."

Mukesh stayed in the dingy place for a week. Then one day the boy informed the police who acted fast and stormed the building and rescued Mukesh from the clutches of the kidnappers.

It was a harrowing experience for Mukesh. He vowed never to trust strangers. He thanked God that he was safe and sound and had escaped from the clutches of the kidnappers and was united with his family. He will never to able to forget this horrifying incident.

HONESTY IS THE BEST POLICY

Sarin was walking along the back lane of a row of shops in town when he saw a bag lying on the road. Someone must have dropped it, he thought. He stopped and picked up the bag. He opened the bag to see if there was anything to indicate who the owner was. Perhaps he could return the bag to the owner. To his utter surprise he found wads of cash neatly arranged in the bag. There must be thousands of rupees in the bag.

Suddenly he heard gruff voices behind him. He turned his head and saw three burly men running towards him.

They quickly surrounded him. The oldest man among the three asked Sarin, "Is that your bag?" Sarin replied, "No I found it on the road". The man again asked Sarin if he had found the bag on the road. "Yes, I found it and was looking inside to see if I could find anything to indicate who the owner is", replied Sarin. "Who are you anyway?" "Police," the man replied taking out an identification bag to show Sarin.

"Then you better take the bag", Sarin said. The policemen took the bag from Sarin and opened it. They showed Sarin what was hidden beneath the money. There were small, small plastic packets with some powdery material in it. Sarin had no idea what the packets contained. "These are drugs", said the policeman.

"Drugs?" Sarin asked in surprise. "Yes we are looking for a known drug dealer who was seen in this area. Our men are all over the place looking for him. It looks as though the dealer has decided to dump the evidence than risk getting caught with it. These is death penalty for those involved in drug trafficking, don't you know?" the man explained to Sarin. After a moment he asked Sarin why he was walking in the back lane. "I am on my way to school Sir," replied Sarin.

"Then you better get going. We have a crook to catch".

Having said that, the men went away. Sarin reflected on what had happened. He could easily have said that the bag belonged to him. There was so much money in it. Had he done that, he would probably be in big trouble by now. The police would have taken him in custody and he could be behind bars. He was glad that he was honest. Honesty is the best policy.

AN INTERESTING JOURNEY

People have been travelling since ancient times in search of job, to visit relatives or just to explore and see the world. Visiting new places is always exciting and adventurous.

The charming, picturesque and beautiful valley of Kashmir is rightly called "Paradise on Earth" and I was fortunate enough to visit it during my summer vacations. It was the month of May and the oppressive heat of Lucknow made life unbearable. My father decided to drive all the way to Srinagar. My mother packed lots of juices and snacks for the fifteen thousand kilometer long journey. We started early from our house in Lucknow.

It was pleasant morning with the breeze blowing gently and the birds twittering on the trees. It took us a good half hour to reach the Lucknow-Kanpur freeway. The farmers were already in their fields. We passed many villages and town. Those small towns are slowly growing up. I could see development projects around them. I suppose one day they will lose their rustic charms and take on the hectic pace of a city. We took our lunch at McDonalds opposite Mathura Refinery. While crossing Now Delhi we were stuck in a jam. It was midnight when we reached Ludhiana, where we checked in a hotel. The next morning we took off to Jammu, a bustling city at the foothills of the Himalayas. While passing through Punjab, we passed fields of sugar-cane, sunflower and mustard. These were many factories manufacturing fertilizers, rubber, shoes and hosiery. There was hardly any rural-urban divide in Punjab. Soon the landscape changed.

The winding roads of the mountains began. The scenery was breathtakingly beautiful as we reached Patnitop. We stopped our car several times to admire the gushing streams, meadows and the snow capped mountains. On one side was the river Chenab with its swift flowing water and on the other side were the deodar, pine and fir trees. We passed a huge dam where hydroelectricity was being generated. After crossing the Jawahar Tunnel we paid the toll tax. A few people were selling cherries and strawberries. We stopped and bought a box each of these, which we enjoyed tremendously for the rest of the journey before they were all gone. The fruit orchards were laden with almonds, cherries and apples.

The spectacular view, the suspension bridges over the streams and the numerous waterfalls all had a calming effect on us. At last, on the third day, we reached Srinagar in the afternoon.

The journey from Lucknow to Srinagar was both exciting, tiring but a memorable one. The beautiful scenery will be always imbibed in my heart for ever.

YOU ARE ALONE AT HOME ONE EVENING STUDYING FOR A UNIT TEST WHEN ALL AT ONCE YOU HEAR A KNOCKING SOUND

It was a hot and humid night in the month of July. My parents had gone for a wedding. I stayed back at home because I was studying for my chemistry test. I was struggling with my studies trying to cram into my head the 'Laws of Chemical

Bonding' and was so engrossed in it that I was seeing molecules floating about in the air. I had no idea that my staying in the house was going to prove so frightening.

It was around 9:30 p.m. when the lights went off. I was just going to light up a candle, when suddenly I heard a noise in the kitchen. I thought it would be a mouse squeaking. Then someone knocked at the door. I was scared. I quickly lit up a candle, but there was no one in sight. There was stillness in the air. The wind was blowing. I looked out of the window and saw lightning in the sky. I got more scared. My hands started trembling. They became cold and clammy. I was shivering and thought of sleeping. So I went to my bedroom and into the bed to calm down. I had a constant feeling that someone was watching me through the window. My heart was thumping. My room was still. The still sound was itching me in my ears.

Suddenly I saw two big eyes peeping through the window. A chill ran down my spine and my heart came down to my boots.

I felt goose bumps and my mouth became dry. My mind became blank. I tried to calm down and quickly took my mobile and called my father, but his mobile was switched off. Someone again knocked at the door. I looked out and again there was no one. I heard sounds of someone walking down the stairs. I thought someone was playing a prank on me, but I was not sure. Suddenly one of the windows of my house smashed against the wall. I stood petrified with fear and my hair stood on one end. As my throat was parched I went to the kitchen to drink water. I felt that someone was standing beside me, yet there was no one. I was frightened and decided to go to my neighbours. What? What? The door was locked. There was no way but to go back. Suddenly the light came on.

My doorbell rang. My parents came in. I heaved a sigh of relief. They saw me sitting in the corner, frightened. I narrated this story to my parents and they had to calm me down with reassuring hugs. I felt my fear ebb away. Slowly my heat began to beat normally.

It was scary. I still wonder who that someone who was disturbing me was. From that time onwards I decided never to stay at home alone.

"THROUGH MY SEMI-CONSCIOUS STATE I HEARD THE DISTANT PEALS OF A TELEPHONE RINGING........"

Through my semi-conscious state I heard the distant peals of a telephone ringing. The cold, dark room was filled with danger and threat. "Is this you?" Thundered the authoritative man with a intimidating voice. A squeamish whimper arose from the dark corner as I tried to concentrate on what the man was saying on the phone. There was a horrifying glare under the man's bushy eyebrows. He reeked of cigarettes.

"Withdraw your name from the elections or your son will die." A sinister laugh came when he finished talking to my father. Gathering my wits, I tried to recall the sequel of events as to how I landed in this mess.

It had been three days since I was captured by three muscular men after school. Beads of sweat dotted my forehead when I saw the glistening blade of knife, used to threaten my safety. For three days, I was locked in this dark and dingy room with hardly any food and water.

"Where am I?"

I questioned myself. Will they ever let me go even after my father withdraws his name from the list of candidates fighting for the election? It seemed impossible, for they looked brutal and cold- blooded. I had to escape if I wanted to live as they tortured and abused me a number of times during the day. Filled with determination, I decided to escape from the clutches of the kidnappers. I glanced carefully around the room. It had high walls. There was only one window, that too at a considerable height. It was impossible to shout for help. Suddenly my eyes fell on a piece of broken glass lying on the floor. I tried my best to crawl near it. After several attempts I succeeded. I picked the glass with trembling hands and started cutting the rope tied to my legs. The rope was strong and thick. It took hours to cut it and at last I was free. But then I heard footsteps coming towards the room. I scrambled frantically and loosely tied the rope around my legs, praying that the kidnappers do not notice it. I covered my mouth with my sweaty palm, struggling to repress my fear. The door opened and a boy of want sixteen entered the room, bringing a plate of rice and dal and a glass of water. He had a gentle and kind face, unlike the man who always came threatening me with dire consequences. My mind was in a whirlpool of chaos, should I ask him for help or not. I gathered courage and asked him if he could help me escape as my only crime was that my father was standing against a powerful minister in the coming election. He remained silent and pushed the plate towards me. I was crestfallen. My only chance to escape had gone.

Two days later the police stormed the building and rescued me. It seemed the boy took pity on me and informed the authorities. In the encounter, one kidnapper was killed. Tears rolled down my checks as the man in khaki uniform held me up and said with a soothing and comfortable voice, "Don't worry, it's all over now".

I was so glad to see my parents. It was such a relief to be safe and free once again

WRITE A STORY ON- 'A BANK ROBBERY'

Manoj, a shrewd, evil man of well-built height is a high school dropout. His father is a dedicated, hardworking I.P.S. officer. His father is an esteemed person in the society and because of this respect, Manoj got selected in an university.

There Manoj met Arpit, a short guy with moustaches, wears dark spectacles and is quick in picking up fights. Piyush is six feet tall, fair and is always arguing with his elders. Rakesh is also the son of a rich business man who is exploiting the resources which his father has provided. Manoj befriends all of them and they become best buddies. They started indulging in bad activities like smoking, drinking and gambling. When their families came to know about their activities they were kicked out of their houses. They dropped their names from the university and exhausted all the money they had in drinking. They started committing minor thefts. On day they decided that they cannot do this and they need a permanent source of income. They were changed souls.

Manoj and Rakesh started working as a clerk in bank in a posh locality.

Piyush started selling newspapers after setting up a stall front of the bank where Manoj and Rakesh worked. Arpit took a catering job and transferred lunch boxes to various offices. They were quite happy with their jobs and felt everything was going as they had desired.

After a week Piyush saw a suspicious man wearing black glasses as he dropped a packet under a chair. Piyush thought it was a bomb and started shouting "Bomb! Bomb!" All of a sudden there was panic on the street. Men were shouting, women were screaming and people ran helter -shelter on hearing the word bomb! People left their cars and ran for safety. Police had sealed the area and had summoned the bomb defuse squad. When the bomb defuse squad opened the packet they found it was empty.

The bomb being there was a hoax. When the bank employees returned to resume their work, they found the whole place ransacked. Money worth 10 crore rupees was stolen. Piyush confessed that the robber was the person who had thrown the packet under the chair. Piyush told the policeman that man was tall and fair. He was wearing a cap. On the basis of this report the police released the sketch leading to several arrests.

One month later Manoj and his friends had quit their jobs and moved in a big bungalow. They had robbed the bank. It was their plan to rob the bank and in which they smartly and cunningly succeeded.

WRITE ON ORIGINAL STORY IN WHICH THERE IS SUDDEN PANIC ON THE STREET WITH MEN SHOUTING, WOMEN SCREAMING AND PEOPLE RUNNING HELTER-SKELTER. WHAT HAS CAUSED THIS SITUATION AND HOW IT IS SOLVED AND WHAT SHOULD BE THE SUBJECT OF THE STORY?

Manoj, a thin ugly boy of fifteen with rough curly hair and baggy clothes was standing in the queue for the school bus.

He was observing the hustle and bustle at the bus station on Alambagh road. Suddenly he caught sight of a peculiar looking man in black trousers and white shirt. The man had a moustache, was of average height and wore dark glasses. Manoj decided to follow him. The man walked with a limp which made Manoj suspicious.

The man kept pacing up and down the street. He had a briefcase and a small bag. He sensed someone was following him. Once or twice he turned his head but was not able to spot Manoj. As the buses kept departing and arriving he kept glancing at his watch. He went near a tree where a scooter was parked. He quickly took out a small silver tiffin box and placed it quietly under a scoter and then took off in a hurry. Manoj lost him in the teaming crowd of passengers who had just alighted from a bus.

Manoj thought there was something fishy about the tiffin box. Could it be a bomb? He had seen on television and heard on the radio that if someone saw any suspicious looking object in public places, the person should at once report to the police.

Manoj ran as fast as he could to the nearly police station and narrated to the police what he had seen. The police at-once swung into action. They cordoned off the whole area and asked the people to vacate the road leading to the bus stand. There was utter confusion as people ran helter-shelter trying to save their lives. Men were shouting and women screaming. People tried to take shelter under tables and wherever they thought it would be safe for them. Ambulance sirens could be heard. People were caught in frenzy and were panicking and running.

The traffic stopped and the police were diverting people to a side road. The officers had evacuated everyone in the immediate vicinity. Eventually the bomb disposal squad arrived. They ran towards the scooter. There were two pipe bombs connected by wires. They carefully took out the wires and the timer. People clapped when it was over. Everyone heaved a sigh of relief. Had the bomb detonated it would have ripped into thousands of pieces- sending out a shock wave of razor- sharp shrapnel, powerful enough to flatten a wide area.

Due to Manoj's alertness, a major tragedy was averted. He was rewarded by the Chief Minister of Uttar Pradesh at a function specially held in his honour and those police officers who assisted in defusing the bomb.

WRITE AN INTERESTING STORY BEGINNING WITH- THREE MEN FOUND A PURSE FULL OF GOLD COINS, WHILE WALKING THROUGH A FOREST

Three men found a purse full of gold coins while walking through a forest. It was a hot summer afternoon and they were exhausted after their long journey. It was a shabby looking purse and one would not have thought they it contained so much wealth.

On finding the coins, the three men who were friends and had left their town in search of employment, were on could nine. They shouted and danced with joy, thinking that all the problems of their lives had been solved. After the excitement had worn out, the three started squabbling over the coins. Greed overpowered them and they soon came to blows as to who would get how much. Since Suresh was wiser then Robert and Mukesh, he suggested that they should count the coins and divide it equally among themselves. "Just two hundred and ten coins"! Mukesh said. "Yes, only two hundred and ten coins", said Robert, counting them again. So they got seventy coins each. They then parted ways.

Mukesh and Robert went back to their town while Suresh set off to Delhi to seek his fortune.

As Mukesh and Robert had not seen so much wealth in their life they fell in bad company. They took to drinking, gambling and cheating very soon. They squandered all their wealth and then started committing heinous crimes. One day while gambling, they had a heated argument. Since both were under the influence of alcohol they came to blows. Enraged that Robert was hitting him, Mukesh wiped out his Coventry- made pistol and fired at Robert, who died on the spot. People caught hold of Mukesh and handed him over to the police. He was charged with murder and sentenced to life imprisonment by the Judge.

On the other hand Suresh who was intelligent and resourceful used his brains. He sold off his share of coins to a jeweler, who after asking him many questions as to how he came in possession of them, very suspiciously bought them. Suresh invested the money wisely. He started his own business and worked very hard to make it successful. Within a span of few years, he became a very prosperous businessman. He bought a nice house for himself to live in. He had fabulous cars and servants who served him faithfully. Every night he would thank God for his good fortune and gave a lot to the poor as charity.

YOU WERE AT AN EVENT ATTENDED BY THOUSANDS OF PEOPLE. GIVE A DETAILED DESCRIPTION OF THE EVENT AND TELL US WHAT YOU DID, THOUGHT AND FELT IN THE LARGE CROWD.

The north London derby is the name of the local derby match played between two north London based football teams- Arsenal and Tottenham Hotspurs. Both Arsenal and Tottenham fans have recognized each other as their biggest rivals and the derby is one of the fiercest in English football. Being an Arsenal fan my uncle had invited me to attend the event during my summer vacations and I could not refuse this golden offer.

The match was played at The Emirates stadium, the home ground of the Arsenal team and just half a mile away from the home stadium of Tottenham. A huge buzz and noise had already developed hours before the stadium. The rival fans stared at each other with hatred and enmity. The club chants were in full swing and being in majority, the Arsenal fans gave the Spurs fans a torrid time and they quickly retreated inside the stadium to their seats. The seat allotment was based on a ratio of 70:30, 70% being the home fans. An hour before the game the players were warming up and all of a sudden the whole stadium was filled with boos. All the fans including me were targeting Adebayor, a former Arsenal player who had joined Spurs for money and as a result his team's manager sent him back to the dressing room after fifteen minutes.

As soon as the players appeared on the field the stadium was echoing with 'Come on you Gooners' chant. Whenever the away team touched the ball, they were jeered and shouted at and their only one monotonous chant could never uplift their team. Around fifteen minutes had passed when the Spurs captain and star defender Vertongen pushed Santi Cazorla and a brawl happened resulting in a number of yellow cards. From the free-kick Sanchez scored and the home fans went berserk. They shouted his name with the announcer and all the home fans continuously shouted at the away fans till half time which resulted in doubling of security near the away fan stand.

After half time the tide had changed completely. We were two goals down. The Judas of Arsenal, Adebayor, had scored a brace and had taken the courage to run around the whole field to celebrate. For the first time, the voice of Spurs fans could be heard. They sang about finishing above Arsenal this year and winning the league. But the Gooners reminded them of their status and mocked them for finishing below us for the last two decades. Arsenal had used all their substitutions and were attacking from every direction. The game came back in our direction after the seventy third minute when Spurs left back, Rose, purposely elbowed Walcott and was dismissed from the game.

The Spurs fans showed their cheap mentality by throwing coins near the goal line area and the ball boy collected the coins with delight. This prompted the Arsenal fans to make further jibes.

In the seventy ninth minute substitute Giroud equalized and within ten minutes the Gunners were 4-2 up. Instead of sticking around the Spurs fans had left early and we all stayed for another half an hour to applaud the players. They also appreciated the crowd support and even signed autographs and took selfies. Unfortunately due to a large number of people I was unable to take any autographs. Every public place in the city was filled with Arsenal chants and the Spurs supporters had retreated to their homes.

Throughout the match I realized that we became a part of the action rather than being just spectators. The audience's reaction is a measure of the team's performance. In the end I was lucky to be the twelfth man on the field.

RIVALRY

"Sharmaji, Run! Run!" The young bodyguards screamed for the slender man. Hundreds of assailants were swarming the motorcade, smashing Rahul Sharma's truck window. But the beloved leader of Jadispur refused to budge.

The mob were supporters of Sharmaji's political rival Dev Das. It was election time and the two were contesting the polls and belonged to different political parties. It was not so twenty years ago when both Sharma and Das were inseparable good friends. People swore by their friendship. Das' father was a member of Parliament. After his father's sudden demise, Das inherited his political legacy and contested the elections. He won and became a minster in the Government. Influenced by corrupt and sycophant advisers, he started taking bribes and commissions in most Government projects and schemes. His supporters held the city to ransom, demanding money, threatening people and unleashing a reign of terror. Fed up with all this, people approached Rahul Sharma to intervene as he was Das' best Friend. Sharmaji tried to install some sense of ethos and honestly in him but in vain. Das had become so conceited and arrogant with so much power and money that he threatened to annihilate his friend if he interfered in his affairs.

Das's ego and haughty behavior surprised Sharmaji. He did not expect this kind of treatment from him. In order to teach his friend a lesson, he joined a political party and actively spoke against his old friend. Not used to opposition from any quarters Das swore to teach Sharmaji a lesson. Once he sent his goons to Sharmaji's house and they ransacked the home and caused a lot of destruction. After this episode the two became bitter rivals.

Sharmaji called a public rally to protest against the malpractices of Das. Thousands of people poured into the streets, to show their resistance against corruption and lawlessness which infuriated Das who ordered the arrest of Sharma for disrupting the peace of the city. Sharmaji spent a week in jail before he was bailed out. Over the years Sharmaji became very popular and was loved by the common people. His simplicity and honesty made him a beloved leader of the masses.

During an election rally, Das's supporters attacked his motorcade. Das knew that if he lost the elections, Sharmaji would set up a committee to probe into all his corrupt deals. Determined to crush his opponent forever, Das sent his musclemen to kill him. Sharmaji's driver somehow got him out of the fray and managed to take him safely to a police station where he lodged a F.I.R. against Das.

After a few weeks the election results were declared and Sharmaji won by a huge margin. The city folks were glad to have got a clean and honest leader after years of suppression and crooked rule.

A ROBBERY IN A RUNNING TRAIN

These days travelling has become unsafe. We read gruesome tales of murder, loot, dacoit almost every day in the newspapers.

During the summer holidays, my friend accompanied by his parents was travelling by Lucknow Mail to New Delhi. They were in the A.C. Compartment. The train left the Lucknow Charbagh Railway station exactly at 10 P.M. It was a night's journey to Delhi. The passengers soon settled down to sleep. At Moradabad several passengers from his compartment got down. It was past midnight, just when the train was about to leave Moradabad station, five young men, aged between twenty to twenty five entered my friend's compartment. They looked like ruffians. They were talking in low and confidential whisper. One of them had a black beard and shaggy eyebrows. The other had a scar under his chin and rough and tangled hair. They all looked tough and wore dirty, smelly clothes. Everyone got alert and they suspected mischief.

Hardly had the train left the platform, the gangsters all stood up brandishing their pistols and other lethal weapons. One of them stood near the alarm chain so that no one could pull it. Another, who seemed to be their leader, cried aloud, "Hands up! Anyone found raising an alarm will be shot dead." They then locked the doors of the compartment.

The passengers were stunned and frightened to death. Cold sweat broke on my friend's face. The robbers handled the passengers roughly and went about the compartment extorting cash and jewelry from every passenger at the point of the pistol. None dared to refuse. Only one young man tried to resist. He was badly beaten up. My friend's father had to part with the few thousands of rupees he was carrying, his watch and his mother with her gold earrings and chain. The hooligans did not spare even the aged passengers. All this took them hardly ten minutes to do their dirty business.

When the scoundrels had finished with their nefarious work, the one standing near to the alarm chain pulled it. As the train slowed down, they jumped off and made good their escape under the cover of darkness. The passengers could hear the trampling of feet as they made their escape. At the Ghaziabad Station, the Railway Police was informed and a complaint was lodged but all efforts to trace them proved futile. The passengers suffered heavy losses but thank God, at least their lives were spared.

A MEETING WITH A GHOST

There are some incidents which one never forgets in life. Some incidents are pleasant while others terrifying.

I remember, it was the month of October. I had gone to visit my aunt who lives in Nainital. Her old rambling bungalow is on a hill. My mother had strictly forbidden me not to venture outside after dark and not to go to the outhouse which was haunted. It was rumoured that there was an invisible intruder in the house, who came night after night.

My aunt showed me a small room with a narrow bed. The window of the room faced the outhouse. I remembered my mother's warning but pooh-poohed it.

I did not believe in ghosts and thought the stories were just to scare everyone. That night, I was sleeping soundly because I was tired from travelling. Suddenly I heard a noise. I pulled the covers over my head, trembling with fear. The light outside my window pierced the incredible pitch-black darkness in the room. The light cast shadows onto the wall. Then came the horrible high-pitched sound of something sliding across the bed room floor, inch by inch, closer to my bed. I cried out "Who's there?" from beneath my covers, gripping my pillow with all my might. An evil laugh echoed throughout the room, as the sound came closer. Through the blankets, I could see an outstretched hand coming towards me. I noticed there wasn't any skin on the fingers, only bones, the bones of skeleton. It seemed to be the ghost of a woman in a long flowing garment. I choked back a scream. The ghost's skin was so white, one could practically see through it. It didn't have a face, only two dark spots where her eyes should be. Her clothes were spookier than a Halloween costume. I sat shaking afraid to move even a muscle. Then the ghost spoke in a cold, harsh voice that she can leave her grave only once every ten years, the week before Halloween. At the stroke of twelve on Halloween night, she must return to her grave. Every ten years, she selects one person from the earth and takes him or her to her grave to become a ghost like her. This year she wanted me. The ghost wants to take me back to her grave to make me a ghost! I ran from the room. I pounded down the hall, jumped off the top step, flying to the ground. "No way!" I said. I raced down to my aunt's room as fast as I could.

I was too frightened to go back to sleep that night. It was a horrible encounter, the memories of which I cannot dislodge from my mind.

MY GREATEST WISH

"If wishes were horses, beggars would ride" goes the old proverb. It is my greatest wish that I become the Prime Minister of India. I will find myself on top of the world if ever I get the coveted post of the Prime Ministership of the country.

India is a vast country with the world's highest population after China. It is blessed with a great civilization and diversified culture. To take care of it efficiently and fulfill the high expectations of the masses as their Prime Minster is no easy task.

My priorities as the P.M. of India will be to remove corruption in every sphere of life, to eradicate nepotism, poverty, illiteracy, over population, communalism and unemployment in the country. I will try to induct only honest and dedicated ministers in my cabinet. I will have ministers who are renowned and successful specialist in the respective fields. With the help of able ministers I will first reform the education system. Everyone who completes their studies would get employment straight away after leaving school as in the countries of Europe and America. There would be free and compulsory primary education for all. Adult literacy classes would be held in the villages and in the urban slums.

My next target would be to eliminate black money and bank deposits of Indians in foreign countries. When I find some people rolling in wealth and the others begging on the streets my heart bleeds. Is this the India of Gandhiji's dream?

I shall develop friendship with the neighbouring countries. If U.S.A. and Canada can keep their boundaries open, why can't we do so with Pakistan and China?

Sufficient funds and facilities would be made available for industries and agriculture. Import and export polices would be reviewed. Industry and farming are inter-dependent. None of them can progress in isolation. Industries would not prosper unless they are provided with sufficient raw material. High quality good seeds, insecticides and latest agricultural tools and techniques need to be made available to farmers for a bumper harvest.

Serious attempts would be made to check population by educating people through the media. The problem of communalism would be tackled by educating the people to follow the best of

Indian traditions and live together in peace and harmony. I shall make India a heaven on earth. This is my greatest wish.

STORY BASED ON THE THEME: 'KNOWLEDGE IS POWER'

'Knowledge comes but wisdom lingers' said Lord Tennyson. Thus with knowledge we get wisdom and with wisdom one can have power and prosperity. People with knowledge wield great power and occupy important position in practically all fields of life.

Suresh was a young man of about thirty years of age dressed in a white kurta pajama. He was of medium height, lean with soft black eyes and an intelligent face. At first glance he looked like any ordinary guy but when he walked to the dais to speak, he impressed everyone present with his in depth knowledge and understanding of problems faced by the common man in his day to day life. When he finished his speech, there were shouts of "Suresh Bhaiya Zindabad". He acknowledged the greetings of the people with folded hands. People garlanded him and showered him with rose petals.

It was Suresh's first visit to his home town after becoming a minster in the newly elected government in the state of Uttar Pradesh. His childhood friend Mukul could hardly hold back the tears in his eyes as he watched him from a distance. He still could not believe that his modest and humble friend had become so famous and powerful, almost like a celebrity.

Suresh's path to glory was not at all easy He had to struggle day and night as he was the son of a poor farmer who could hardly earn enough money to support his family. There were times when Suresh went without food as there was nothing in the house. He somehow finished his schooling in his village and later went to Lucknow for higher education. His maternal uncle supported his college expenses and then he won a scholarship and got a master's degree in agriculture from Lucknow University.

Unlike other youths, Suresh returned to his native village, to put his knowledge to practical use, for the benefit of the villagers. His family and friends rebuked him for wasting his time in the village instead of taking up a job in the city. Unperturbed by criticism, he continued to work on the small patch of land his father owned applying his knowledge to improve the yield of his crop.

In two years he bought more land. His scientific method of farming soon caught the attention of the villagers. They came to him for advice and he readily helped them. He became very popular. To improve the lot of the villagers, he formed self-help groups. He developed a proper drainage system for the village and drew the attention of the district authorities to install hand pumps in the village. Suresh taught the villagers how to produce gobar gas from cow dung. Thus in no time he transformed his village into an ideal village having all the basic amenities. His good work and popularity caught the attention of a political party who gave him a ticket to contest the election. He won with a huge margin and emerged victorious.

It was Suresh's knowledge which set him apart from the ordinary and he was thus able to command power. Thus, this story truly illustrates the proverb "Knowledge is power".

WRITE A STORY ON: YOU CANNOT CLIMB THE LADDER OF SUCCESS WITH HANDS IN YOUR POCKETS

Once upon a time in Chandanpur, there lived Seth Ramjidas who was famous for his status, wealth and power. He was a workaholic who had built his business empire from ashes and dust. Ramjidas not only controlled the businesses of the city but gave advices on matters of disputes.

Seth Ramjidas had only one son, Mukuldas. Being the only son he was given all the care and affection which made him a lazy fellow. Mukuldas had a rough start in school. He used to say two plus two is twenty two, picked up fights regularly and only passed due to his father's power. His so called education finished and he became an arrogant, boorish, indolent and an irresponsible man without an aim in his life. Seeing his son's condition, Seth Ramjidas fell ill and passed away leaving all his wealth to his son. Mukuldas said that God will carry on the business for him. Slowly the family income started dwindling. Many employees became independent, broke his clients and took over the shops.

All this did not affect Mukuldas. He was still earning a meager amount and was satisfied with it. The famous family lost its glory and importance. People started looking down upon Mukuldas and he became a source of jokes and an example of someone not to be for everyone. Mukuldas was earlier unaffected by all this but slowly these things made a significant impact on him. He realized how foolishly he had lost importance, wealth and power. A spirit to rise once again made him ambitious.

Mukuldas took all the employees to the court who had illegally taken over his shops. Soon he got his shops back. He publically humiliated those people who had taken credit from him and took them to the police and obtained double the amount. He worked hard and eventually took over all the business activities which were his father's wishes. He fought the local elections and emerged victorious with a huge margin. Mukuldas looked after the people and expanded the business empire to many cities. His construction firm built malls, hospitals, hotels and he led an expedition to discover an oil well as well. By the time he reached sixty he had become the country's richest man.

Mukuldas's hard work and sheer desire to succeed transformed him from a rude, lazy fellow into a generous, workaholic, man. He was awarded many times by men of great honour. When he died, his sons carried on the tradition; and the family name and honour has become the backbone of the tradition of Chandanpur.

STORY ON A RIVALRY BETWEEN A FATHER AND SON

Once upon a time in the city of Udhampur lived Seth Tadoridas. He was a shrewd businessman and a corrupt politician. He controlled all the business activities of the city, made changes which benefitted his business and did all his best to destroy any rivals. Seth Tadoridas was a five time MLA who bought the voters, got the elections rigged and indulged in all sorts of corrupt activities.

He had only one son, Kejridas. Being the only son he was showered with all the blessings but his father ensured that he never became a spoiled brat. Tadoridas provided him the best education and sent him abroad for higher studies. There Kejridas' mind opened. Education had reformed him and broadened his mental outlook. He wanted to transform his father so he returned to Udhampur after completing his studies. He tried to tell his father about the bad deeds he was doing and there was still enough time for him to change. Tadoridas threatened his son and told him not to interfere in his affairs.

Failing to convince his father, Kejridas joined his father's rival political party. He started raising the voice of the people whom his father had destroyed, gave interviews regarding his father's corrupt practices and even sat on 'dharnas' to ensure justice for the people. His movements and speeches started motivating people and he became popular with the citizens. Tadoridas would hardly believe that his son had become his rival and cursed himself for educating his son.

The elections were coming near and the father and son were giving their best to defeat each other. They exchanged heated arguments and threw various allegations against each other. Tadoridas said in one of his rallies that he had kicked his son out of the house because he used to gamble, drink and steal and that his son was not an angel but Satan himself. Kejridas publically opened up his father's methods of buying votes. He requested the people to take the money but vote for him.

Tadoridas did not want to lose against his son. He hired miscreants and assassins to kill Kejridas. All these methods and antics failed. Tadoridas invited him for one on one debate in which he accused and humiliated his son of treachery and betrayal and warned the voters about his ugly side.

The voting day passed and everything remained normal and quite but the situation turned volatile when the results were declared. Tadoridas had lost badly. He called the results false and demanded re-elections.

Kejridas used all his forces to stop all this and started an organization to look into all the scams done by his father. Soon his father was arrested and sent to jail. Kejridas remained to be a fan favourite and under his leadership Udhampur became the richest city in the country.

A MEETING WITH AN ALIEN

"Nabola, Nabola Zisco Dabola Iliwan Visco Zabulu. Li Vi Chabo Mitra Vatro."

"Oh! I'm very sorry Earthling. I really forgot that you did not speak Titara language. Hello, hello, my name is Viscolishiula Zabulu. I have come here to explore the beautiful planet of yours. I have seen the wonderful waterfalls, mountains, flowers and fruits in your planet. It is for sure that this planet has the most beautiful sites of nature. Our planet Chabon is millions of light years away from Earth. It was barren at first but efforts have been made to convert it into the most beautiful planet in the universe. It seems nitrogen and oxygen is found in abundance on Earth. We live on Krypton gas which is scarce on Earth, so I have to carry a Krypton gas tank for my survival. We have very unique and supernatural powers. We can fly and become invisible. I have come to observe and study you Earthlings, know about your habits, your occupations and of course your behaviour. You Earthlings are very different from us. We are green in color with a metallic outer covering. I have been on Earth for the past one day, 17 hours, 34 minutes, to be exact. One thing is for sure that you Earthlings are very backward in science and technology. We have explored countless number of galaxies, numerous planets and everything concerning the universe. We know all about our planet and its history, its structure and all other things, but you Earthlings are far behind us. You haven't even explored the whole Solar System. We have also discovered fascinating things which help us in our daily lives, for example you Earthlings grow your food and cook it before eating, but we all chew small tablets with relish which provides us with all the nutrients. Everything on our planet is computerized but you people still do half of your work manually. Our modes of transportation are compact jet like vehicles which zip through the air and are eco-friendly."

"One major difference between you and us is that we all Chabonan's are united. We never use the word 'I' like you. Peace and prosperity rules on our planet. There hasn't been a single war among us, but on Earth there have been hundreds of wars, including two World Wars. I have also learnt that the countries are still invading each other. It is a pity to see you Earthlings engaged in these futile wars. We can only pray to God that peace prevails on this beautiful planet Earth."

"As for me, I am going back to my home planet, Chabon, where my people will be waiting for me. So, goodbye and thank you for the memories."

Made in the USA
Columbia, SC
24 July 2018